TASTY BIBLE STORIES

TASTY BIBLE STORIES

A Menu of Tales
& Matching Recipes

TAMI LEHMAN-WILZIG

ILLUSTRATIONS BY
KATHERINE JANUS KAHN

KAR-BEN
PUBLISHING

To the important people in my life:

– My father (of blessed memory) and my mother (may she continue to enjoy long life), whose combined genes formed the recipe for my writing talents. I am forever grateful.

– Sam, who always knows how to cook up the right blend of support and love. Thank you for your critiques, encouragement, and for being the ideal spouse.

– Boaz and Avihai, the spice of my life.

–TLW

To my mother, Edmina Benish Janus, whose creative, imaginative cooking gave me great happiness all the years of her life.

–KJK

Text copyright © 2003 by Tami Lehman-Wilzig
Illustrations copyright © 2003 by Katherine Janus Kahn

KAR-BEN PUBLISHING, INC.
A division of Lerner Publishing Group
241 First Avenue North
Minneapolis, Minnesota 55401 U.S.A.

Website address: www.karben.com

Library of Congress Cataloging-in-Publication Data

Lehman-Wilzig, Tami.
    Tasty Bible stories : a menu of tales & matching recipes / by Tami Lehman-Wilzig ; illustrated by Katherine Janus Kahn.
      p.   cm.
    Summary: Retells 14 familiar Old Testament stories in up-to-date language with related recipes.
    ISBN 1–58013–080–1 (pbk. : alk. paper)
    1. Bible stories, English. 2. Cookery—Juvenile literature. [1. Bible stories—O.T. 2. Cookery.]
I. Kahn, Katherine, ill. II. Title.
BS551.3.L44 2003
221.9'505—dc21   2002151697

Manufactured in the United States of America
1 2 3 4 5 6 — DP — 08 07 06 05 04 03

Contents

Hungry?

BITE INTO SOME DELICIOUS STORIES.

Have you ever seen a yummy-looking cookie or smelled something that made you really hungry? If so, then you're no different from most people in the Bible.

In the beginning, you will recall, all it takes is a juicy piece of fruit to get Adam and Eve in trouble.

And the smell of the stew that Jacob is cooking is *soooo* good, Esau offers to exchange his birthright for a bowl.

When does Queen Esther tell the king that wicked Haman is planning to kill all the Jews? During the feast she invites everyone to attend. The queen understood that people are in a better mood and more willing to listen when they're eating good food.

Can you think of other Bible stories related to food? Peek into the pages of this book and you'll find many more.

Read them and then try the recipes. Some of the recipes are easy to follow, while others require an adult by your side, so get your family into the kitchen. You'll have a lot of fun together and before you know it, all of you will be cooking with the Bible and enjoying food fit for the kings and queens of Israel.

Kitchen Safety

Wash all fruits and vegetables well before you begin to prepare.

And don't forget to wash your hands, too.

Make sure an adult is present when you do the following:

Use a blender or food processor.
Chop or cut foods with a sharp knife.
Open a can and/or drain liquid from a can.
  (The lid has sharp edges.)
Fry in hot oil.
Cook on a hot stove.
Drain hot water from pasta.
Pour hot liquids.

Eat and Enjoy!

EVE: THE APPLE OF ADAM'S EYE

After God created the heavens and the fields of the earth there was no one to till the land. So God created Adam. He was the center of the universe, a very important guy!

"I want to make life as pleasant as possible for you," God told Adam, "so I've given you this exclusive estate, the Garden of Eden."

The garden was beautiful to look at and full of trees bountiful in fruit. Two trees stood in the middle of the garden: the Tree of Life and the Tree of Knowledge.

"You can eat from every tree except for the Tree of Knowledge," God instructed Adam. "If you eat from that tree, you will die."

"No problem," said Adam.

But there was a problem. Adam was lonely. He had no one to share his life. So God caused Adam to fall asleep. While he slept, God created Eve from one of Adam's ribs. When Adam awoke he saw a woman before him and he was pleased to have her love and friendship.

Unfortunately, another creature hopped onto the scene—a sly serpent determined to trick Eve.

"What's there to eat?" the serpent asked Eve.

"We can eat the fruit of all the trees except for the Tree of Knowledge," she replied.

"Not so," the cunning creature answered. "You can eat from that tree. Your eyes will be opened wide, and you will see the difference between good and bad, just like God."

It sounded logical to Eve, and the fruit did look juicy and delicious, so she picked a few and ate them. They were so yummy that she picked a few more and gave them to Adam, who also gobbled them up.

Unfortunately, God saw everything and got very mad. "Why did you do this?" God bellowed at them.

"She made me do it," Adam whined, pointing to Eve.

"It made me do it," cried Eve pointing to the serpent.

"Who me?" The serpent looked surprised.

"Yes, you," insisted Eve. "You're a sneak . . . You're a snake . . . You're a sneaky snake."

"You disobeyed me," boomed God, "and for that there will be consequences."

"You," he hollered at the serpent, "you will no longer have legs. You will have to crawl on your stomach for the rest of your life and your offspring will have to slither as well."

"Speaking of offspring," God growled at Eve, "because you didn't listen to me, you will experience great pain when you give birth to your children."

Finally, directing his anger at Adam, God declared, "And you, Adam, you will no longer be treated to a Garden of Eden. From now on, you will have to farm a land full of prickly thorns and thistles."

So God sent them out from the garden.

Adam and Eve were the first to learn the difference between good and bad. As for the luscious fruit, we're not sure of the exact variety. While some say it was figs, most believe it was apples. Certainly, Eve was the apple of Adam's eye, and at first she didn't give a fig about what God had commanded. Here are two easy recipes: a baked apple with raisins, and fresh figs and sour cream.

BAKED APPLE Á LÀ MODE

1 serving

Ingredients

1 medium Golden Delicious apple

1 tsp. sugar mixed with ¼ tsp. cinnamon

1 Tbsp. raisins

1 heaping Tbsp. of the ice cream of your choice

Step-by-Step Preparation

1. Core the apple, leaving a deep hole in the middle.
2. Sprinkle sugar-cinnamon mix inside and around the top of the apple.
3. Fill the hole with raisins.
4. Microwave on high for three minutes.
5. Let cool, then fill with ice cream and eat.

FRESH FIGS AND SOUR CREAM

5 servings

Ingredients

5 fresh figs cut in half

½ cup sour cream

3 heaping Tbsp. finely chopped walnuts

½ cup raisins

Step-by-Step Preparation

1. Place the cut figs on a dish.
2. Top with sour cream.
3. Sprinkle with chopped walnuts and top with raisins. Serve.

NO SOUR GRAPES FROM NOAH

Many years after God created Adam and Eve, the earth was full of wicked people. God was not pleased and decided that it was time to start all over. The trick was finding someone to rely on. Thankfully, one man named Noah was a good and honorable person.

"Listen, Nice Noah," God said one day. "Soon I'm going to bring a terrible flood. No one will survive except for you, your family and two of each kind of animal."

"Oh my!" cried Nice Noah. "What do I have to do?"

"Don't worry," answered God in a soothing voice. "You are a farmer, but I'm going to teach you how to be a carpenter so that you can build a giant ark and go with the flow." God gave Noah step-by-step instructions, and soon he, his family and each animal pair set sail.

Now Noah was a calm person. Very little annoyed him—not even living with hundreds of animals for 40 days of pouring rain! Even being stuck in the ark on top of Mt. Ararat for another 150 days didn't get him angry, but it did make him curious. He opened the ark's window to take a peek.

"What do you think, boys? Should we send out a raven to find out if the flood is over?" he asked his sons Shem, Ham and Japheth.

"It's not a bad idea, Father," they replied.

Out went the raven. It flew back and forth, forth and back, waiting for the waters to dry up.

When more time had passed, Noah asked, "Maybe we should send out a dove this time?"

"You have nothing to lose," his sons answered.

The dove understood it had been given an important job. It proudly saluted Noah and flew off. Shortly after, it came back.

"No place for me to land," the dove panted. "It's wet everywhere."

Noah waited another seven days before sending the dove out again. This time the dove came back with a freshly-picked olive leaf in its mouth.

"Wonderful!' cried Noah. "The land has dried up and the fruits have begun to grow." Holding the olive leaf in his hand, Noah realized he had the first ingredient of Mediterranean cooking.

God told Noah to leave the ark and to bring his family and all the animals with him so they could be fruitful and multiply.

Excitedly, he cried out to his family, "Let's go!"

Now able to farm again, Noah was interested in growing new fruits.

"I have a grape idea!" he called out happily one day.

"You mean GREAT idea," corrected Shem.

"No, I mean GRAPE," insisted Noah. "I'm going to grow grapes!"

So Noah planted the world's first grapes, which turned into the world's first vineyard, which began the world's first wine industry. Here's a grape recipe for you to prepare, plus another using the olives from the branch the dove brought back.

"GRAPE" FRUIT SALAD

4–6 servings

Ingredients

3 oranges

2 bananas

2 apples

1 cup grapes

½ cup raisins

½ cup orange juice

1 tsp. finely chopped almonds (optional)

Step-by-Step Preparation

1. Peel the oranges, bananas and apples.
2. Cut the bananas into thin slices. Cut the oranges and apples into small cubes.
3. Place the cut fruit in a bowl, add grapes, raisins and orange juice, and mix.
4. Sprinkle finely chopped almonds on top and serve.

3-BEAN OLIVE SALAD

6 servings

Ingredients

½ can pitted green olives

½ can pitted black olives

1 can string beans

1 can chickpeas

1 can kidney beans

1 cup cherry tomatoes

1 large onion

¼ cup olive oil

2 Tbsp. lemon juice

pepper to taste

Step-by-Step Preparation

1. Drain the liquid from the canned vegetables.
2. Pour the olives, string beans, chickpeas and kidney beans into a bowl.
3. Cut cherry tomatoes in half and add them to the mixture.
4. Cut the onion into thin slices and add them to the mixture.
5. Add olive oil, lemon juice and pepper, and mix.
6. Chill before serving.

SARAH
THE FIRST HOSTESS
WITH THE MOSTEST

Generations after Nice Noah and his family began to repopulate the earth, there lived a man named Abram, who was a descendant of Noah's son Shem. Abram lived in the land of Ur where he met and married a very beautiful woman named Sarai.

Abram and Sarai were a happy couple. Unfortunately, one thing was missing from their lives—children.

One day God appeared before Abram.

"Abram, I know that you and Sarai are disappointed that you have no children," said God. "Trust me. Everything will work out. One day the two of you will be the father and mother of a huge nation."

"Is that a joke?" asked Abram.

"Trust me," repeated God.

Years went by. Finally, when Abram was 99 years old, God appeared again.

"Remember that promise I made to you years and years ago? That you and Sarai would be the parents of a huge nation?" God asked Abram. "Well, it's time to sign a contract."

"Do you know how old Sarai and I are?" questioned Abram.

"I believe in late bloomers," God assured him. "From now on your name will be Abraham and Sarai's will be Sarah. The two of you will start a new nation that will have millions of people."

Abraham sat in front of his tent thinking over everything that God had said to him, when three strangers appeared. Always happy to have guests, Abraham invited the men inside.

"Please come in and wash your feet," Abraham urged them. "I'll be right back with something to drink and eat."

Abraham rushed into the tent calling out, "Sarah! We have company!"

"They must be fed," Sarah answered immediately, showing she had the makings of a Jewish mother. "I'll quickly make some cakes while you roast a calf," she instructed.

Abraham set the meal in front of his visitors.

"Umm, delicious," they agreed. "Where is your wife Sarah?" they asked Abraham.

Abraham immediately became curious. "Why do you ask? Do you want to compliment her on her cooking?"

"That, too, but we want to tell her that we'll be back for more delicious food in nine months time when we come to celebrate the birth of your son."

Standing at the tent's door, Sarah heard the men talk and laughed to herself, "A mother at my age!"

Even though Sarah couldn't believe her ears, she did know that if and when the time came, she would happily prepare a festive meal.

Perhaps this Biblical Breakfast was what Sarah served when baby Isaac was born, as predicted, nine months later!

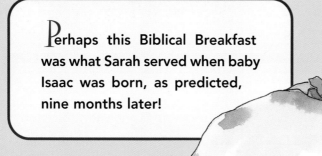

BIBLICAL BREAKFAST MENU

Pita pockets

Tehina sauce

Hummus

Yogurt

Granola

Freshly-cut vegetables

Apple juice

FILLED PITA POCKETS

8 servings

Ingredients

4 large pita breads

2 medium cucumbers

2 medium tomatoes

1 small onion

2 Tbsp. chopped parsley

Sprinkling of olive oil

Hummus (ready-made or recipe below)

Ready-made tehina (optional)

Step-by-Step Preparation

1. Cut the pita breads in half to make two pockets.
2. Dice washed, unpeeled cucumbers finely. Put them into a bowl.
3. Finely chop the tomatoes, onion, and parsley and add them to the bowl.
4. Sprinkle olive oil on the salad and mix thoroughly.
5. Open each pita pocket. Spread hummus on the inside, then fill it with salad.
6. If you like tehina, add a teaspoonful on top. Eat and enjoy!

HOMEMADE HUMMUS

Serves 12 or more when used as a dip

Ingredients

1 can chickpeas

1 cup tehina paste (not ready-made tehina)

1 tsp. salt

2 tsp. chopped parsley

1 tsp. chopped green onions

Paprika and garlic powder to taste

3–4 tsp. lemon juice

Step-by-Step Preparation

1. Drain the can of chickpeas. Save juice.
2. Empty the chickpeas into the food processor or blender.
3. Add all other ingredients and blend until smooth.
4. For an even smoother consistency, slowly add the chickpea juice until you reach the desire texture. Remove from the food processor and serve.

IN A STEW OVER A BIRTHRIGHT

Although they were twins, Jacob and Esau were as different as different can be. Rugged and hairy, with a ruddy complexion, Esau was the outdoors type. He loved to hunt and be out in the fields. Jacob, on the other hand, was a quiet person who liked to stay at home and think. He also liked to cook. In fact, he did his best thinking while cooking.

One day, Jacob was cooking a thick, tasty stew when Esau came home absolutely starving.

"I'm home and I'm hungry," Esau called out, smelling the stew's inviting aroma. "What is there to eat, and where is that fantastic smell coming from?"

"Over here, brother. It's a new stew that I'm trying out."

"Look, I'm dying from hunger. Give me some quick," insisted Esau.

"Not so fast," replied Jacob.

"I've had a hard day, I feel as though I'm going to faint, and you say 'not so fast?' What kind of brother are you?"

"A brother who wants to make sure that we both get our just rewards."

"What are you getting at?" Esau was very confused.

"Look," explained Jacob. "I know that Father considers you the eldest because you were born one minute before me."

"That's right. Respect your elders," growled Esau.

"I respect you," answered Jacob. "I admire your hunting capabilities, and I think you're a great sportsman, but I don't think it's fair that because you're one minute older you should inherit twice as much of Father's property. Why does this birthright belong to you?"

"Is that what's bothering you?" Esau couldn't believe his ears. "My birthright! You can have it. Just put some food on my plate."

Jacob couldn't believe what he was hearing. "You mean," he asked, "you'll give me your birthright for a bowl of my stew?"

"You've got it," agreed Esau. "Is it a deal?"

"It's a deal," answered Jacob. "You swear?"

"I swear," declared Esau.

Jacob poured some lentil stew into a bowl and gave it to Esau along with some bread. Why did Esau find the stew so satisfying? What made its aroma so inviting? To find out, try this recipe. Afterwards treat yourself to a lentil dip.

JACOB'S LENTIL STEW

This dish gets thicker and tastier each time you reheat it.

12–16 servings

Ingredients

1–2 cups brown lentils (use more for a thicker stew)

½ cup barley

½ cup red kidney beans

2 medium onions

2 medium carrots

2–4 potatoes (use more for a thicker stew)

2 fresh garlic cloves, crushed

4 heaping Tbsp. powdered soup mix

8 quarts water

Pepper to taste

1–2 lbs. cubed beef or veal (optional)

Step-by-Step Preparation

1. Wash the lentils, barley and kidney beans, and place into a pot.
2. Coarsely chop onions and add them.
3. Peel and slice carrots, and add them.
4. Peel and cube potatoes, and add them.
5. Add the garlic, soup powder, pepper and meat cubes.
6. Fill the pot with water and stir contents. Bring to a boil. Turn down heat and simmer for 2 hours. Stir every 15 minutes. Serve hot.

SPICY LENTIL DIP

Ingredients

1 cup lentils

3 cups water

2 Tbsp. ready-made tehina

2 tsp. soy sauce

1–2 Tbsp. tabasco sauce (add slowly and taste until it's spicy enough for you)

2 tsp. lemon juice

1–2 Tbsp. garlic-pepper (add slowly and taste)

Step-by-Step Preparation

1. Soak the lentils in water for 2½ hours. Drain.
2. Bring 3 cups of fresh water to a boil, add the lentils, lower the flame and cook until the lentils are soft (about 45 minutes)
3. When lentils cool, drain them, and place them in a food processor with other ingredients. Blend until smooth.
4. Serve as a dip with crackers, or spread inside pita bread before stuffing it with kebab or shwarma.

JOSEPH FEEDS HIS FAMILY

Joseph couldn't believe his eyes. It had been 20 years since he had last seen the tired and hungry-looking men standing in front of him. Yet, he immediately recognized them to be his jealous brothers who had sold him into slavery when he was a young boy.

"I am the governor of Egypt," boomed Joseph. "What can I do for you?"

The nervous brothers bowed. One meekly stepped forward and explained, "We've come from Canaan, where there is no food. We have an old father and a large family that we must feed. We hear that you have corn and we would like to buy some."

Joseph smiled inside. He was happy to hear that Jacob, his father, was still alive. But there were only ten brothers standing in front of him. Where was his youngest brother Benjamin?

"Are you ten brothers?" he asked.

"Actually we were twelve," came the answer. "One of our brothers is dead, and the youngest is back home with our elderly father."

"Prove to me that you are not spies," Joseph demanded.

"How?" they asked in unison.

"I'll give you sacks of food to take back, but one of you must stay here in prison until you return with your youngest brother."

The brothers knew they had no choice if they wanted to eat. They left Simon in Egypt while the others returned to Canaan.

When they arrived home, the brothers told Jacob of their journey and the governor's request that they bring Benjamin back to Egypt. Though Jacob feared that something terrible would happen to his youngest son, he agreed.

"You're back," smiled Joseph, when he saw his brothers upon their return. Cradling Benjamin's chin in his hands, he added: "This must be your youngest brother, and you must be hungry after your journey. Please join me at my house for a meal."

The brothers were scared. Who were they to eat side-by-side with the governor of Egypt?

At the end of the meal, Joseph had their sacks filled up again. He instructed his servant to hide a silver cup in Benjamin's sack.

"Thanks for your hospitality," said the brothers, eager to make their way back home. They hadn't gone very far, when they heard the hoofs of horses following them.

"Stop!" called out the rider. "The governor demands that your sacks be searched. A silver cup is missing from his household. Whoever has the cup in his sack must become the governor's servant."

When the cup was found in Benjamin's sack, Judah tried to convince Joseph to keep him instead of Benjamin. "Our father cannot bear to lose his youngest son," he pleaded.

Joseph asked his servants to leave the room. He gave Judah a penetrating stare. "You still don't recognize me," he said. Facing all his brothers, he smiled and said, "Relax. Nothing's going to happen. Remember that annoying little brother who was always showing off? Kid brothers are a real pain, and here I am giving you problems once again."

"What?" they gasped. "Joseph???!! Are you . . ."

"Yes, it's me. Now we're even."

Joseph was full of surprises and here's a surprise for you. Did you know that the ancient Egyptians invented pasta? Little wonder. Joseph had instructed them to store grain for the coming famine so they learned to do something creative with it. Try this pasta salad recipe and another grainy Middle Eastern salad called Tabouleh.

PASTA SALAD

8–10 servings

Ingredients

1 package fusilli (spiral pasta)—preferably tri-color

Italian dressing

1 can tuna fish

2 tsp. mayonnaise

2 hard-boiled eggs

6 pickles

10–15 cherry tomatoes

3 slices yellow cheese of your choice

2 carrots

Step-by-Step Preparation

1. Prepare the pasta according to the directions on the package. Drain, rinse in cold water, and drain again.
2. Place the pasta in a large bowl. Sprinkle it with Italian dressing and mix.
3. In a separate bowl, mix the tuna with mayonnaise, then add to the pasta.
4. Slice and add the hard-boiled eggs and the pickles.
5. Cut the cherry tomatoes in half and add them.
6. Cut the cheese into small pieces and add.
7. Add more Italian dressing to taste and mix.
8. Peel carrot strips into the salad and mix one last time. Serve chilled.

TABOULEH

8–10 servings

Ingredients

2 cups cracked bulgur wheat

Boiling water to cover

4 tomatoes

6 green onions

2 Tbsp. chopped dill

1 cup chopped parsley

2 Tbsp. chopped mint

3 Tbsp. olive oil

4 Tbsp. lemon juice

1 tsp. salt

¼ tsp. pepper

Step-by-Step Preparation

1. Place the cracked bulgur wheat in a large bowl and cover with boiling water. Let stand for 30 minutes until the water is absorbed.
2. Seed and finely chop the tomatoes and green onions.
3. Once the wheat is ready, mix together all the ingredients.
4. Refrigerate and serve cold.

BITYA SAVES BABY MOSES

Years after Joseph died, the Children of Israel had grown into a large nation ruled by a new and wicked Pharaoh.

"Hebrews here. Hebrews there. Hebrews everywhere," said Pharaoh to his advisors. "We can't do without them, but we can't do with so many of them." Pharaoh stroked his pointed beard, raised his eyebrows and ordered, "Tell the midwives to kill all the newborn male Hebrew babies."

News of Pharaoh's order spread fast. When an Israelite woman named Yocheved gave birth to a son, she tried hiding him for three months. "It's no use," she said one day to her daughter Miriam. "I can't hide your baby brother any longer. I'm too afraid."

"I have an idea," answered Miriam. "I hear that Pharaoh's daughter Bitya is as good-hearted as he is evil. Rumor has it that she goes down to the Nile every morning to bathe. Let's build a small ark for our baby and float it down the river so Bitya will find him. A woman so kind will fall in love with a baby as beautiful as he."

That evening, Princess Bitya invited her handmaidens to eat and stock up on food for their families. "Egypt is blessed," she told them. "The banks of the Nile flood each year and water our crops, giving us plenty of fruits, vegetables and wheat. Come girls. Fill your sacks."

When they finished, Bitya bid them goodnight. "Don't forget our early morning swim in the Nile."

While Bitya was sleeping, Yocheved and Miriam busily built an ark out of bulrushes and tar, making it as comfortable as possible. As the sun rose, they gently put the baby inside the ark, carried it down to the river and set it afloat in the direction of Pharaoh's palace.

"How can we be certain your plan will work?" Yocheved asked.

"Don't worry, Mother. I'll follow the ark. As soon as the baby is in safe hands I'll come back to you."

Miriam walked along the banks of the Nile, listening to her brother whimper. As she neared the palace she heard girls giggling and splashing. Hiding behind the bushes, she saw Bitya and her handmaidens bathing.

"This is fun," the maidens giggled.

"Why then do I hear the sound of tears?" asked Bitya.

As the girls fell silent they heard a whimper that grew louder and louder. "It sounds like a baby, but . . ."

Suddenly a tiny ark floated into view. When the princess saw the baby, it was love at first sight. "Who does he belong to?" she wondered aloud.

Miriam revealed herself. "It is a Hebrew baby. Shall I get a wet nurse to feed him?" she offered.

Bitya accepted. "Bring the woman to my palace."

While Miriam ran to get her mother Yocheved, Bitya took the baby home.

"Bitya, what will you call the baby?" asked one of her handmaidens.

"I'll call him Moses, because I drew him out of the water."

Bitya's family now had one more mouth to feed. What kind of food did they eat? The ancient Egyptians had a very rich cooking tradition. Did you know that they were the first to make mayonnaise? Have a meal fit for the Pharaohs. Try this mayonnaise recipe as well as a typical Egyptian egg dish and a fresh salad.

MAJESTIC MAYONNAISE

Ingredients

1 egg

2 Tbsp. wine vinegar

1 tsp. white wine

½ tsp. salt

1 tsp. sugar

pepper to taste

1½ cups vegetable oil

Step-by-Step Preparation

1. Place all ingredients except oil into a bowl. Using an electric mixer, blend at medium speed.

2. Slowly add oil and blend until thick. Use in recipes that call for mayonnaise.

EGGPLANT OMELET

1 large or 2 small servings

Ingredients

½ small eggplant
oil as necessary
½ small onion
3 eggs
1 tsp. chopped parsley
1 tsp. chopped dill
salt & pepper to taste

Step-by-Step Preparation

1. Cut the eggplant into cubes. Sprinkle them with salt and let stand for 30 minutes. Then rinse the cubes and pat them dry.
2. Fry the eggplant in oil until golden brown. Drain on a paper towel.
3. Chop the onion and fry it in the same pan.
4. Beat the eggs in a separate bowl. Add the eggplant cubes, the parsley and dill, fried onion, salt & pepper.
5. Pour the mixture into a frying pan. Cook on a low flame until the omelet is set. Serve immediately.

"FATOOSH" BREAD SALAD

2 servings

This is a fun recipe where you use the pita bread as an edible plate.

Ingredients

2 pita breads
1 large cucumber, unpeeled
1 tomato
1 small onion
1 tsp. chopped dill
½ small head of lettuce, shredded
1 Tbsp. lemon juice
2 Tbsp. olive oil
salt & pepper to taste
6 fresh mint leaves, chopped

Step-by-Step Preparation

1. Put each pita bread on a napkin. Gently flatten it.
2. Cube the cucumber, tomato and onion and place with lettuce and dill into a bowl. Mix them together.
3. Spoon the mixture on each pita bread.
4. Mix the lemon juice, olive oil, salt & pepper and sprinkle the dressing over the salad on each pita. Sprinkle with chopped mint.

GOD PASSES OVER THE JEWISH HOUSES

Moses was on a work break. Delivering plague after plague to the Egyptians was a difficult job. He couldn't understand why God had so much confidence in him.

"Pharaoh's one tough nut," he commented to his brother Aaron.

"God told you he was going to make Pharaoh's heart turn to stone," reminded Aaron.

"Still," insisted Moses, "look at all these horrible plagues: the Nile water turning to blood, frogs jumping all over the place, fleas in everyone's hair, hail raining down from heaven, darkness for three days and nights. It's a little tough to take."

"A lesser man would have caved in a long time ago," agreed Aaron.

"Yes," reflected Moses. "I hope this last plague will do the job."

Moses thought about his life. From a baby floating in an ark of reeds down the Nile, he had grown up to be a prince among the Egyptians.

"The good life, I knew it well," he admitted to Aaron. "Twenty years ago I never would have believed that I'd leave all those riches behind. Now, with this final plague, I'm going to close the circle."

Moses was referring to Pharaoh's decree that first-born Hebrew boys be drowned in the Nile. His sister Miriam and his mother Yocheved had saved him. Now, in order to free the Hebrew slaves, God was going to kill all the first-born in every Egyptian household.

Moses shivered at the thought. "That Pharaoh! If he hadn't been so hard-hearted until now, we wouldn't have to bring this horrible plague upon the Egyptians," he told his brother.

"Come, we have a job to do," urged Aaron. "We must gather the Children of Israel and instruct them on how to make sure that God passes over their homes."

The elders listened carefully as Moses provided them with step-by-step instructions.

"On the 10th day of this month," he began, "every family must bring home a lamb. On the 14th day they must kill the lamb and smear its blood on the side posts of their front doors, so that God will know it is a Hebrew home. Afterwards, they should roast the lamb over a fire, make unleavened bread, and eat them with some bitter herbs.

"Finally," concluded Moses, "see to it that everyone is fully dressed, wearing sandals, and that the head of each family has his walking stick in hand."

"Why?" asked the elders in unison.

"We must be ready to leave Egypt at a moment's notice," Moses replied.

"Anything else?" asked the leader of the elders.

"Yes. Tell the people that this feast is the beginning of a tradition," Moses declared.

"Tradition?" the elders sang out in unison.

"Tradition," answered Moses. "Once we get out of here, every year at this time, the Children of Israel will celebrate their freedom by eating unleavened bread for seven days."

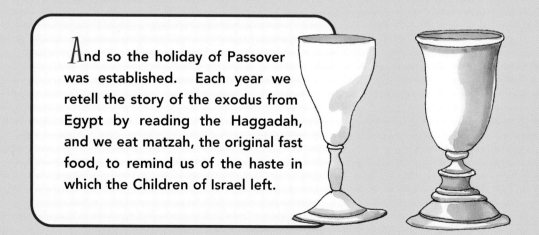

And so the holiday of Passover was established. Each year we retell the story of the exodus from Egypt by reading the Haggadah, and we eat matzah, the original fast food, to remind us of the haste in which the Children of Israel left.

GOOD MORNING MATZAH BRIE

2 servings

Ingredients

2 pieces of matzah

milk for dipping

¼ stick (2 Tbsp.) margarine

¼ cup sugar mixed with 1 tsp. cinnamon

Step-by-Step Preparation

1. Pour the milk into a bowl. Break the matzah into large pieces and soak them in the milk.
2. Melt margarine in a frying pan. Add the matzah. Sprinkle with the cinnamon mixture and fry for a minute. Turn the matzah over and sprinkle again with the mixture. Fry for another minute. Serve hot.

GRANNY FANNIE'S COLD EGG SOUP

6 servings

Ingredients

6 hard-boiled eggs

3 cups cold water

salt to taste

Step-by-Step Preparation

1. Peel the eggs, cut them into pieces and place them in a bowl.
2. Add the water and mix until the mixture turns yellow.
3. Add salt to taste.
4. Refrigerate. Serve cold.

CHAROSET

Ingredients

2 medium Golden Delicious apples

2 medium Granny Smith or other tart apples

½ cup finely-chopped almonds

¼ cup sweet wine

¼ cup dry wine

1 Tbsp. cinnamon

Step-by-Step Preparation

1. Peel and core the apples and grate them into a bowl.
2. Add all the other ingredients and mix.
3. Refrigerate for 3–6 hours. Place on the seder plate to eat with matzah and maror.

GRUMBLING IN THE WILDERNESS

When the Hebrew slaves got to the Sea of Reeds, Moses stretched out his hand. The water parted, forming a path for them to cross.

"Hooray for Moses; he did it!" they shouted.

"Hooray for my brother; he's some leader!" sang Moses' sister Miriam.

"Hooray for God; we couldn't have done it alone," reminded Modest Moses.

"Yes, yes," everyone agreed. "God is on our side."

But once they had their freedom, the Children of Israel were not so grateful. Walking through the wilderness was no picnic, and they started missing the basic comforts they had enjoyed in Egypt.

"My lips are so dry," complained some.

"What do you expect," whined the others. "There's no decent water to drink; it's too bitter."

"My God!" called out Moses. "Only three days in the wilderness and already they're complaining."

"We'll have to quench their thirst," God said, showing Moses a tree. Moses broke off a branch and tossed it into the water, and the water became sweet.

"Drink up folks," commanded Moses.

You'd think the Children of Israel would quiet down after this. Well, they didn't complain again—for a month-and-a-half. Then. . . BOOM!

"Our stomachs are growling," they grumbled. "Enough foraging for berries. After a hard day's wandering we need some bread. We can smell the aroma of those fresh loaves we used to eat in Egypt. And what about some protein? Where's the beef? We're h-u-n-g-r-y!!!!!"

"Listen to them grumble!" exclaimed Moses to God.

"Don't worry," answered God. "Every day we'll have a storm, but instead of water, it will rain bread. They can collect their daily portion."

"What if they complain that man cannot live by bread alone?" Moses continued.

"I haven't forgotten that they want meat as well. Gray clouds will gather at dusk and I'll send a meat storm every evening. They'll have a quail of a time."

"You mean whale of a time," corrected Moses.

"No, that's Jonah . . . but his story comes later. I mean quail. That's the bird I'm going to send. Run along, tell Aaron, and spread the word among the people."

No sooner did Moses and Aaron finish their announcement, when a heavy black cloud appeared in the sky and the rain began. In the evening quails fell from the sky, and in the morning, flakes as fine as frost covered the ground. The Children of Israel looked at this strange substance and asked, *Mun Hu?* ("What is this?")

It was mun – a type of bread they had never seen in Egypt – what we today call manna (in Hebrew, a "portion"). Biblical commentators say that it tasted like whatever the eater wanted it to taste like. You might say that manna was the original tofu. You make of it what you want to.

Pretend that you're one of the Children of Israel wandering in the wilderness. Hungry? Think about the manna and quails when you make these delicious tofu recipes.

SCRAMBLED TOFU

1 serving

Ingredients

1 small onion
2 Tbsp. oil
4 oz. hard tofu
¼ tsp. ground ginger
¼ tsp. dry mustard
¼ tsp. garlic powder
salt & pepper to taste

Step-by-Step Preparation

1. Chop the onion and fry in oil until golden brown.
2. While the onions are frying, cut the tofu into small pieces.
3. Add the tofu to the fried onion, sprinkle the seasonings on top and continue frying. Stir the mixture.
4. Serve when the tofu gets golden brown.

OPEN-TOASTED TOFU SANDWICH

1–2 servings

Ingredients

2 slices white bread
4 thin slices of tofu
2 tsp. olive oil
1 medium tomato, thinly sliced
2 tsp. basil
salt & pepper to taste

Step-by-Step Preparation

1. Toast the white bread.
2. Place 2 thin slices of tofu on each piece.
3. Spread 1 tsp. of oil on top of the tofu.
4. Cover with tomato slices.
5. Sprinkle basil on top and then sprinkle salt and pepper to taste.
6. Put the open-toasted tofu sandwiches in the microwave and heat on high for 45 seconds. Eat and enjoy.

HUNGERING FOR EGYPTIAN FOOD

Two years after leaving Egypt, the Children of Israel were still wandering and still complaining. They discovered that being one large family wasn't very much fun.

"Why did we leave Egypt?" they cried out. "What made us think that life would be better as free people?"

"Just listen to them," demanded Moses of his brother Aaron. "These are the same people we're supposed to turn into a nation so that we can live in our own land? And God hinted our wandering could last forty years. I don't know if I'll be able to stand it."

"Building a nation takes time." Aaron put his hand on his brother's shoulder. "And being the father of this nation certainly is a hard job. But you've got me to lean on."

"You're a good guy, Aaron." Moses smiled and patted Aaron on the back. Just then, the complaining started up again.

"Enough of this manna," the people cried. "Mun oh Mun, we want something more to eat."

"Let's go hear what they're complaining about now," sighed Moses.

"Fish . . . we want fish!" cried out a group of men.

"What kind?" called out another group.

"The kind we had in Egypt, what do you think?"

"Tuna?" giggled some women. "We didn't have that in Egypt, but we do know a good recipe."

"Stop joking," demanded the first group. "What about some of those delicious fresh vegetables and fruits that grew along the shores of the Nile? Like cucumbers. And leeks, and onions, and garlic for added taste. Our mouths are watering just thinking about them."

"And what about those big, fat, juicy watermelons?" added a lone voice.

Moses scolded the complainers. "For God's sake, are you at it again?"

"Speaking of God," piped up one Israelite. "You know how to reach him. Give him our shopping list. Remember, we want fish, cucumbers, leeks, onions, garlic and watermelon . . . and don't forget the meat."

Moses was fed up with all the complaining, but he understood how the people felt. "Oh God, what have I done?" he called out to the Lord. "I've taken these people out of slavery and made them miserable. It's too much for me to handle alone."

"You're not alone," God answered. "I want you to gather seventy elders and bring them to the meeting tent."

"Now I have to have a town meeting?" Moses balked.

"I will appear before them in the same way that I appear before you," assured God. "And then I'm going to give them a piece of my mind. Being a free people is worth a lot more than fish, cucumbers and onions."

You guessed it. God ignored the shopping list. Still, the Children of Israel never forgot the fresh vegetables and melon they ate in Egypt. When you try these recipes, you'll understand why their mouths watered.

SPICY CUCUMBER & GARLIC SALAD

4 servings

Ingredients

3 large cucumbers, unpeeled

3 garlic cloves

1 small hot red pepper

¼ cup olive oil

Step-by-Step Preparation

1. Cut the cucumbers into small cubes. Place in a jar.
2. Peel and finely chop the garlic cloves. Add them to the jar.
3. Cut open the hot pepper (you may want to wear gloves) and remove the seeds. Finely chop the pepper, and add to the jar.
4. Pour the oil into the jar. Cover and shake. Refrigerate for several hours. Serve cold.

TUNA SPREAD

2 servings or use as a dip

Ingredients

1 can tuna

1 hard-boiled egg cut in pieces

1 heaping tsp. chopped parsley

½ small onion, cut into quarters

1 Tbsp. mayonnaise

Step-by-Step Preparation

1. Drain the tuna and place it in the food processor.
2. Add the egg, chopped parsley, onion and mayonnaise.
3. Blend until the mixture is smooth.

YOGURT-TOPPED WATERMELON

6–8 servings

Ingredients

1 small watermelon

2 cups vanilla-flavored yogurt

Chocolate sprinkles

Step-by-Step Preparation

1. Slice and cut the watermelon away from the rind, and cut into medium-sized pieces.
2. Pour the yogurt into a separate bowl.
3. Dip a watermelon piece into the yogurt, then sprinkle it with chocolate and eat.
4. If you have a fruit scoop, you can cut the watermelon in half, scoop out watermelon balls and place them in a bowl. Top the balls with yogurt and sprinkle with the chocolate.

THE SPIES CHECK OUT CANAAN

God was not happy that the Children of Israel constantly complained, but understood their frustration.

"They have a lot of growing up to do before they become mature enough to be a nation," God assured Moses. "In the meantime, let's give them something to look forward to, to make their lives exciting."

"Personally, I've had enough excitement," replied Moses.

"Relax, I don't mean more miracles," God said. "I mean mystery. Let's do some spying."

Moses smiled. "You never stop surprising me with your ideas."

Following God's game plan, Moses invited one man from each tribe to a meeting.

"Listen up, we've got important work to do," he began.

"Yeah, like getting us out of this wilderness," they answered.

"Exactly," smiled Moses. "Our aim is to settle in the land of Canaan. The only problem is, we don't know what Canaan is like."

"What does that have to do with us?" asked one of the tribesmen.

"Everything," answered Moses. "Your job is to go to Canaan and find out all there is to know about it."

"That sounds like Mission Impossible!" they all cried out.

"No," corrected Moses, "it's Mission Very Possible."

"What kind of information do you want?" they asked.

"Find out if the people living there are strong or weak," instructed Moses. "Tell us how they live—in cities or in camps. And. . .most important," winked Moses, "tell us what kind of food they eat. Bring back a whole menu for us to look forward to."

Everyone's mouth started to water. This was a job they all had an appetite for. The spies saluted Moses and marched off.

When they arrived in Canaan they discovered the first grapes were ripe. They cut a large and luscious branch to bring home for "Show & Tell."

"Take a look at the big, juicy pomegranates . . . and the figs," called out one of the spies. "I can't wait to sink my teeth into one of these!"

It took forty days for the spies to do their job. They all agreed that Canaan was a land flowing with milk and honey. But that wasn't the whole story that they brought back.

"Moses, don't even ask about the food. There's plenty of it, and it's delicious," they reported.

Moses raised his eyebrows. "Then what should I ask about?"

"The people," whispered one spy. "They're real, live giants. We look like a bunch of grasshoppers next to them. There's no way we'll be able to beat them in a battle."

Two of the spies, Caleb and Joshua, didn't agree. "Have you forgotten that God is on OUR side?" reminded Joshua.

"NO, NO, WE WON'T GO!" insisted the other ten spies. "And we'll tell our people not to go as well."

"Psst, Moses. Over here," God beckoned Moses. When they were alone, God let loose his anger. "I've had it!" God hollered. "This group doesn't deserve to live in Canaan. They can stay in the wilderness for another forty years. I don't give a fig. Only Caleb and Joshua will enter Canaan with the next generation."

And that's exactly what happened. Only the next generation was allowed to enjoy the foods of Canaan, the land of milk and honey, grapes, pomegranates and figs. You can enjoy them by trying out these recipes.

PULPY GRAPE JUICE

3–4 servings

Ingredients

1 cup green grapes

½ cup light raisins

4 tsp. sugar

3–4 cups water

Step-by-Step Preparation

1. Wash the grapes and raisins and soak them in water overnight.
2. The next day, place them along with the sugar in a blender, add water, and blend until the mixture reaches a juicy, but pulpy texture.

HONEY-SWEET CARROTS

4–6 servings

Ingredients

1 12 oz. bag frozen carrots

Water to cover

1 cup light raisins

1 cup dark raisins

2 Tbsp. cinnamon

2–3 Tbsp. honey

Step-by-Step Preparation

1. Bring the carrots and water to a boil, lower the heat and add the raisins.
2. Add the cinnamon and honey and stir well.
3. Cover the pot and simmer for 20 minutes.

A SLEEPY GLASS OF MILK

God allowed Moses to take a peek into the Promised Land from the top of a mountain, but it was Joshua who led the Children of Israel into Canaan and helped them defeat their enemies.

Centuries passed, and the Children of Israel were now ruled by a series of judges, among them a woman named Deborah from the tribe of Naftali.

Deborah was not only a judge, she was a prophet. She understood the difference between right and wrong, and warned others of the consequences. A modest woman, Deborah held court under a palm tree.

One day, Deborah thought about the situation of her people. The Children of Israel currently were at war with the Canaanites. Both nations insisted that the land belonged to them. It was a difficult war since a very smart and mean general named Sisera led the Canaanites.

Deborah was feeling sorry for the Children of Israel when suddenly she had a prophetic vision. God would confuse Sisera, and the Israelites would win. She wasn't sure exactly how it would come about, but she had the feeling a woman would play a role in this victory.

Deborah called for Barak, the head of the army. "Barak, I know there's a war out there and we're getting slaughtered, but I've just had a vision, and we're going to win."

"Women . . ." smiled Barak. "You're great as mothers, but you'd better leave the fighting to us."

"I beg your pardon," snapped Deborah. "In case you've forgotten, I call the shots. And my better judgment tells me that you have to go up to the top of Mount Tabor and look the enemy straight in the eye."

"Who me?" quivered Barak. "I don't think so . . . at least not alone. You come with me."

Deborah led Barak up the mountain. Just as she predicted, the Children of Israel easily defeated Sisera's troops.

"Go catch him," Deborah commanded Barak, pointing to Sisera as he fled.

But Sisera was too quick for Barak. He slipped off his horse and ran through the hills. He spied a tent and rushed toward it. Hearing the beat of Sisera's feet, a woman named Yael came out of the tent and greeted him.

"Sisera, I'm so honored to see you," she said softly. "Please come into my tent and rest."

Sisera didn't know how to be kind. "Bring me some water . . . now! I'm thirsty!" he barked.

"Who does this guy think he is?" Yael said to herself. "I'm not going to walk miles to the nearest well."

She turned to Sisera and smiled. "I have something better," she assured him, pouring a glass of warm milk. "Drink this. It will help calm you down."

Sisera gulped down the delicious milk. Within minutes he was fast asleep. "Nighty, night, you creep," whispered Yael, "I have something to make your sleep so deep, you'll never wake up."

Yael took a hammer, removed a peg from her tent and hammered it into Sisera's head, killing him.

Hours later, Yael once again heard footsteps. When she went out of her tent she found herself face to face with Barak.

"I think the man you are looking for is inside my tent," she smiled slyly. Deborah was right. It was a woman who succeeded in killing Sisera.

What kind of milk did Yael serve Sisera? Was it from a goat or a cow? No one knows for sure, but everyone agrees that warm milk is tasty and soothing. If you're hungry and tired, eat a sandwich with goat cheese spread, and drink a cup of hot milk with cinnamon. It will fill your tummy and soothe you.

HOT MILK WITH CINNAMON

1 serving

Ingredients
1 cup milk

½ tsp. cinnamon

1 cinnamon stick

Step-by-Step Preparation
1. Pour the milk into a microwaveable cup. Stir in the cinnamon.
2. Microwave for one minute.
3. Remove, stir with the cinnamon stick and drink.

GOAT CHEESE SANDWICH SPREAD #1

2–3 servings

Ingredients
¼ cup soft goat cheese

2 tsp. sesame seeds

1 tsp. sweet paprika

Step-by-Step Preparation
1. Add the sesame seeds and paprika to the cheese and mix thoroughly.
2. Spread on sliced bread and eat.

GOAT CHEESE SANDWICH SPREAD #2

2–3 servings

Ingredients
¼ cup soft goat cheese

2 tsp. sliced green olives

1 tsp. dill

Step-by-Step Preparation
1. Add the olives and dill to the cheese and mix thoroughly.
2. Spread on sliced bread and eat.

RUTH REAPS HER REWARD

Decades later, a great famine broke out, as bad as the famine during the time of Joseph. With nothing to eat, many Israelites decided to move. One of them was a man named Elimelech.

"Naomi," he said to his wife, "let's try our luck in the fields of Moav. I hear they have plenty of food there."

So Elimelech, Naomi and their two sons moved from Bethlehem to Moav. Poor Elimelech died shortly thereafter, and Naomi was left with her two sons and their Moabite wives. Her life became even more bitter when her two sons also died suddenly.

Naomi called her daughters-in-law to her side. "Orpah, Ruth, I have decided to return to Bethlehem. Moav is your home, not mine. You stay here and remarry. I will return alone."

Orpah decided that Naomi was right and kissed her mother-in-law goodbye.

Turning to Ruth, Naomi said, "Go. Go with Orpah."

"No," Ruth said firmly. "When I married your son I became part of your people. Your God is now my God, and I will live wherever you decide to live."

"Stubborn girl," scolded Naomi, even though she appreciated Ruth's loyalty.

Together Naomi and Ruth returned to Bethlehem. Poor and tired, Naomi did not look the same as when she had left years before.

"Don't worry," Ruth said soothingly to Naomi, "I won't have to beg for food. I'll gather the leftover grain in the fields. Do you know any landowners who are especially kind?"

"I do," answered Naomi, remembering that her husband had a relative who owned a lot of land. "There is one man in particular. His name is Boaz. He is a respected man in the community."

"Then I'll certainly go to his fields to glean wheat," smiled Ruth.

Later that day, when Boaz went out to his fields, he saw Ruth and asked his workers who she was.

"That's the Moabite woman who came back with your cousin Naomi," they answered.

Boaz appreciated Ruth's devotion to Naomi. Calling her over, he said, "I don't want you playing the field. Stay only on my land and follow my men."

At the next mealtime break, Boaz told Ruth to sit with his reapers.

"You must be hungry," he insisted. "Have some bread and dip it into this sour wine." Then Boaz turned to his workers and instructed them to leave as much barley and wheat as possible for Ruth to glean.

When the harvest was over Naomi realized that Ruth's future lay with Boaz. More than that, Naomi felt that Ruth and Boaz were made for each other. Both were kind. Both were gentle. And both were wise.

"Tonight I want you to dress in your best clothing," Naomi instructed Ruth. "I want you to look as beautiful as a princess. I want you to make Boaz realize that he can't live without you."

And that's exactly what happened. Ruth married Boaz and they lived happily ever after. Ruth may not have been a real princess, but she did become the great-grandmother of the great King David. Pretend that you are sharing a meal with Ruth or Boaz by following these barley and rye seed recipes.

BARLEY & ONIONS

6 servings

Ingredients

1 large onion, chopped

2–3 Tbsp. olive oil

boiling water

1 lb. package of barley

2 Tbsp. chicken soup powder mix

2 Tbsp. parsley

Step-by-Step Preparation

1. In a deep pot, fry the onion in olive oil until golden brown.
2. Boil a kettle of water.
3. Add the barley to the onions and continue frying, adding more oil if necessary.
4. Pour enough boiling water over the barley to cover.
5. Add the soup powder mix and parsley, and stir.
6. Cover the pot and simmer until the barley absorbs all the water. Fluff with a spoon and serve hot.

CARAWAY SEED CABBAGE SALAD

6 servings

Ingredients

1 package of washed and shredded cabbage

1 large onion, finely chopped

4–6 Tbsp. caraway seeds

3 Tbsp. lemon juice

¼ cup olive oil

Step-by-Step Preparation

1. Place the shredded cabbage into a bowl. Add the onions and caraway seeds and mix.
2. Pour in the olive oil and lemon juice. Toss the cabbage mix.
3. Refrigerate and serve cold.

DAVID MISSES THE NEW MOON FEAST

Ruth's great-grandson David was a young shepherd when King Saul first met him. He loved music and played the harp while tending his sheep.

Word of David's musical talent spread so far that soon King Saul's servants heard about him. Their king, who was forever at war with the Philistines, had a bad temper. When they heard about David, they realized they may have found a way to calm Saul.

They cautiously called to their master, "Oh King Saul, we know you don't like being mad all the time. If you had a good harpist to play by your side, you'd relax and feel better."

King Saul raised his eyebrows, intrigued.

"Find me a harpist NOW," he bellowed, "or I'll have something else to harp about!"

And that's how David entered King Saul's court.

In the beginning, he played the harp and carried Saul's armor. Later, David proved to be a great warrior. Twirling a net filled with stones, he challenged the nine-foot giant Goliath:

"Hey Goliath, you're only a stone's throw away!" he chided. Then David aimed at the giant's forehead and killed him. The Philistine army turned and ran in fright.

"Now that's so impressive that I'm going to make you the commander of my troops," the king told David

David was on top of the world. The king appreciated him, the king's son Jonathan had become his closest friend and the people of Israel adored him.

"David is OUR hero," the Israelites called out.

But that was the last thing King Saul wanted to hear. Aside from having a bad temper, he was also a very jealous man.

"David is a threat to my throne," he confided to Jonathan. "Something must be done about him. Tomorrow is the feast of the new moon. Make sure David comes."

Although Jonathan loved his father, his friendship with David was more important to him. Jonathan understood that the king planned to kill David at the feast.

"You're in great danger, my friend," Jonathan warned David. "My father heard the people praise you, and he's convinced that you'll become king instead of him. To stop you, he's going to kill you tomorrow at his new moon feast.

"The feast lasts for two days," explained Jonathan. "You will hide in a place that only the two of us know. If you're still in danger when it's over, I'll send you a sign to stay in hiding."

The next day the animals were sacrificed, the table was set with beautiful glasses and dishes, and the shofar was blown, calling everyone to the feast.

Saul saw that David's place was empty. "Where's David?" he asked.

"He had to go to Bethlehem to be with his family for the new moon feast," answered Jonathan.

"You're up to no good," Saul accused him. "You love David more than me."

On the third day Jonathan sent David a sign to stay in hiding. David was grateful, even though he had missed some yummy meals like these. Start with easy-to-make mock chopped liver. Serve a main course of meatballs in soy sauce on a bed of rice with chickpeas.

MOCK CHOPPED LIVER

6 servings

Ingredients

1 large onion

2–3 Tbsp. olive oil

1 lb. can string beans

1 lb. can chickpeas

2 cups shelled walnuts

Step-by-Step Preparation

1. Chop the onion and fry in oil until golden in color.
2. Drain the cans of beans and chickpeas and pour into a food processor. Add the fried onion and shelled walnuts, and blend until smooth. Chill and serve cold on a bed of lettuce or spread on crackers.

MEATBALLS IN SOY SAUCE

4–6 servings

Ingredients

3 cups tomato juice
1 onion, chopped
¼ cup soy sauce
1 lb. ground meat
1 egg
¼ cup ketchup
¾ cup flavored breadcrumbs

Step-by-Step Preparation

1. Place the tomato juice, chopped onion and soy sauce into a medium size pot and bring to a boil.

2. While the sauce is heating, place the ground meat into a bowl. Add the egg, ketchup and breadcrumbs. Mix all the ingredients with your hands, until they blend together.

3. Once the sauce boils, lower the heat. Roll the meat into small balls and gently place each one into the pot. Cover the pot, raise the heat and cook for 1 hour.

4. Stir the meatballs every 20 minutes, so they cook evenly. Serve on a bed of rice with chickpeas.

RICE & CHICKPEAS

4–6 servings

Ingredients

1½ cups uncooked rice
3 Tbsp. oil
3 cups water
4 Tbsp. ketchup
1 lb. can chickpeas
salt & pepper to taste

Step-by-Step Preparation

1. In a pot, lightly fry the rice in oil until slightly golden in color.

2. Add the water, cover the pot and cook on medium-high until the water is absorbed. Stir the rice every 5 minutes to keep it from sticking.

3. Once the water is absorbed, fluff the rice.

4. Drain the juice from the can of chickpeas. Add the chickpeas, ketchup, salt and pepper to the rice, mix together and serve.

QUEEN ESTHER'S FEAST

Hundreds of years after King David, the land of Canaan was conquered by the Romans, and the Jews were forced to leave. Some moved to Persia, where a king named Ahashverosh ruled.

Ahashverosh liked to entertain. "Let's have a party," he often commanded his servants, who quickly invited all the nobility to a grand banquet. Back then a party lasted for days!

Once, after a week of partying, Ahashverosh — who had drunk too much wine — summoned his wife Vashti so that everyone could see how beautiful she was.

But Vashti had a mind of her own. "I'm sick of parties, and I don't like being put on display. Tell the king 'forget it,'" she balked.

"Who does she think she is?" roared the king. "If she doesn't come I'm taking the crown away from her."

Poor Vashti. That was the end of her reign.

Ahashverosh decided to hold a beauty contest to pick a new queen.

Among the beautiful young women brought to the court was Esther, the niece of Mordechai the Jew.

"You're more beautiful than anyone else," Mordechai advised his niece. "Don't tell anyone you're Jewish, and I'm sure the king will choose you."

Mordechai was right. King Ahashverosh fell in love with Esther and made her his queen.

Shortly after, the King appointed a new Chief Minister. He was Haman, a wicked man who hated the Jews.

One day when Haman was walking by the palace, he saw Mordechai sitting at the gate.

"Hey-man," called out Mordechai.

"You mean Haman," he sternly replied.

"Hey, Haman, congratulations on your promotion," Mordechai said.

"Bow down before me," Haman ordered.

"In your dreams," answered Mordechai.

Haman, who was steaming mad, went straight to the king and pleaded, "My Lord, there is a people living among us who do not obey the laws of the land. They must be destroyed."

"Do whatever you feel you have to do to save my kingdom," answered Ahashverosh.

Haman ordered that on the 13th day of the month of Adar, all Jews were to be destroyed and their property taken.

Mordechai understood that only Esther could save Persia's Jews.

"Pray for me," Esther asked. "I'm going to fast for three days, then I'll go to the king."

On the third day of her fast, Esther put on her royal dress and went to the king. Seeing Esther made Ahashverosh happy.

"I have prepared a feast and I would like you and Haman to attend," Esther smiled.

Ahashverosh and Haman came to Esther's feast. After they had eaten her delicious food Ahashverosh asked, "Is there something on your mind?"

Esther shocked the king with her answer. "If you love me, then let me live. An evil man wants to kill all of my people. Therefore I too shall die."

The king was furious. "Who is this man?" he demanded.

"Your most trusted adviser," Esther answered, pointing her finger at Haman.

"You," the king blustered. "Guards!" he called out. "Take him away and hang him."

And so Esther saved her fellow Jews. She understood that the way to her king's heart was through his stomach. We don't know what she served at her feast, but here are some Persian recipes for you to make. Start with a fresh herb mezze. The word comes from the Greek word *maza* which means mixture. In Persia the mezze is an appetizer. Mix and match your own fresh herbs, or try this suggested recipe.

FRESH HERB MEZZE

2 servings

Ingredients

2 slices of the bread of your choice
2 tsp. each parsley, mint, green onion and dill
sprinkling of olive oil
salt and pepper to taste

Step-by-Step Preparation

1. Sprinkle one teaspoon of each herb on each slice of bread.
2. Top with olive oil and salt and pepper to taste.

PERSIAN RICE

8 servings

Ingredients

2 cups uncooked rice
1 Tbsp. olive oil
salt to taste
½ tsp. turmeric
4 cups water

Step-by-Step Preparation

1. Lightly fry the rice in olive oil until golden. Mix in the salt and turmeric.
2. Add the water, cover and bring to a boil. Lower heat and cook until the water is absorbed. Stir occasionally to keep from sticking. When the water is absorbed, turn the stove off and fluff the rice.

PERSIAN KEBAB

3–4 servings

Ingredients

1 small onion, chopped
¼ cup lemon juice
6–8 chunks of beef or lamb kebab
garlic powder

Step-by-Step Preparation

1. In a bowl, combine the onion and lemon juice and mix.
2. Sprinkle the meat with garlic powder, then marinate in the lemon mixture for 30 minutes.
3. Grill or broil the kebabs on both sides and serve on a bed of Persian rice.

INDEX OF RECIPES

METRIC CONVERSIONS

Mass (weight)

1 ounce (oz.) = 28.0 grams (g)

8 ounces = 227.0 grams

1 pound (lb.) or 16 ounces = 0.45 kilograms (kg)

2.2 pounds = 1.0 kilogram

Liquid volume

1 teaspoon (tsp.) = 5.0 milliliters (ml)

1 tablespoon (tbsp.) = 15.0 milliliters

1 fluid ounce (oz.) = 30.0 milliliters

1 cup (c.) = 240 milliliters

1 pint (pt.) = 480 milliliters

1 quart (qt.) = 0.95 liters (l)

1 gallon (gal.) = 3.80 liters